Flesh

ESSENTIAL POETS SERIES 254

Canada Council
for the Arts

Conseil des Arts
du Canada

ONTARIO ARTS COUNCIL
CONSEIL DES ARTS DE L'ONTARIO

an Ontario government agency
un organisme du gouvernement de l'Ontario

Canadä

Guernica Editions Inc. acknowledges the support of the Canada Council
for the Arts and the Ontario Arts Council. The Ontario Arts Council
is an agency of the Government of Ontario.

We acknowledge the financial support of the Government of Canada.

Flesh

Sonia Di Placido

GUERNICA
EDITIONS
TORONTO • BUFFALO • LANCASTER (U.K.)
2018

Friends ... 49

Greener ... 63

The Moon and Her Friends ... 83

Quia Paterfamilias
Avis, Cogentilis

Prologue

A Poet Makes Noise

with *her or his* sleeve
cotton inked
noise brushing
at nerve damage

A Pencil scribbles
noise *lead*ing sharp(er)
signals outside
pulped wood.

Trinity

In a dream he founded iPads
glowing from the arms of Moses

hold the book   a flat screen
in your hand

the way you embrace all the babes
the flesh of this planet

consider their three skins
Book-Baby-Handscreen

their spines together
a new breed of shapeshifter

pulping retina
polytherian   vertebrate

The Akashic Wood

And now we roam in Sovereign Woods
And now we hunt the Doe
And every time I speak for Him—
—Emily Dickinson

The Wood belongs to the Father
—Kate Greenstreet

I

Father Forensic,
You won't say your name,
only "I am that I am.
Why should we hurry Home?"
but how to live that way —
Why love anything?

II

Sprawling steel fences
40 years rusteen
aligned to 1969 and 1971
Homeland Security found
mapped in farm divisions

The MOB of WOP is
foot-dipped in concrete
A CN Tower erect
        late(her) comes
its colossal open dome.

III

I am not wanted tongue tasting the cedars.
Sweet-potato squashed placenta,
Samnite* princess coagulating home.
A panino and a salted dried Prosciutto,
late night Bonomelli chamomile tea.

IV

Omega Motherland can't love,
Alpha Fatherland won't love.
But you love everything
Singing Oracular to Saints.

V

I stand in airports collecting 3 carts
lugging luggage to customs
with cheese and customs before 9/11
wandering in and out of
visitations to waterfalls:

Niagara
      Smiths
            Chippewa
                  Iguazu
                        Kagawong, Bridal Veil

                    Americas Fatherland.

VI

Forgotten olive tongues
tenderized moose
dead duck dinners
loon(ied) identity squawking —
a verbose cult of culture:
7 biblical days
in a psychiatric hospital.

A tower above treaty
dome without roof.

VII

The drive to Thunder Bay
clicks with rubber wheels over
cement roads.
I vibrate like an oboe ring
above highway pelts.

No highway tar is smooth under
the Chevy Oldsmobile, 1979.
The bubbled fermenting wine
trunk clucks like we are in
a-basements.

VIII

Anglers angled to the doe kill.
Rifle shots in Winchester Walnut
steel 22" barrel Kimber rifled.

Where is the skating rink
on a hunter's camp site?

No pardons once the horned moose
calls a wild birch bark cylinder song.

IX

That's not going to change
the stench of wild innards,
wet fur skins adjacent to Cantina,
wine sweat, fur trade — taxidermies
watching the Native squalor. (American SP)

Strega had claimed me
from the 18th year of Levi's jeans,
baby denim wash, corrupt slave cotton,
mounted moose antlers, stuffed deer heads,
ducking ducks in glassed cabinets.

X

Damned Forest Hunt Parley —
Parlay — console the dead:
*"A taxidermist can't mount
in the Akashic Wood!"*
That's where you are —
freeze-framed in oak armoires.

The charming chimes
of a grandfather clock,
my mausoleum museum
parlor. (American SP)

Trailer Words for Wooing in the Woods

It's naked, not nude.

It's not cruel; it's crude.

Canto for a Cameo Trailblazer

The pine needles fall
like an axe in the forest
Can you hear them crumble?
　　—Jack Spicer

In a quest for the quiet, low-carved ivory bond,
(a ring) carrying a cameo of colonial
penitence among a consecrated catholic earth,
I shape shift to become him — a fanatic fan
for the West, the benign exotic trailblazer,
a spoor in foreign(er) forests — a novel tramp
adopting hooves. The W-I-D-E-R WILD.
He gives me the gift of the Piscean, the fabulist,
a subject of Neptune's fantasist. Because
I walk through these alien branches, I have
scratched out my heart to become the familiar
territory, so that the old grape vine talks with broken
leaves of birch, deciding to become deciduous.
So that her grapes exchange priory, where the virgin
ingénue sleeps, and the excellence of Juno's marriage
to the handsome Cypress, the taller phallic, comes
to converse with Jack Pines in frost. Tracking the slab
no-stone sidewalks, as if cement were the advance
to the Akashic wood, to blaze the edges of trails,
I hear the moon groan. Her still orbit above urban lampposts
by night. The flatter lakeshore city sewage pouts,
missing its stars; this is where I am left. The remainder is
a thousand years' Diana's warrior returned to greet
a concrete mathematic, God's Arm-strong in space.
He repairs fabled epics for physics, appeases the mind —

its perpendicular grids and trysts: latitude and longitude.
I awaken here to recall the smells of ripe acorns, dried
needles, rotten twigs crumbling into groves spreading
their hardened brown seeds. The spines depraved of green
light, frisking in the wind to fortune by way of Ground Zero,
gathering their sum and sod from composed clusters into
compost they oppose the *intaglio* of my human imprint.
I touch these cameos, carving my sight and sense, become
the gem-like stone background reborn into canto.

Field Notes from a Taxidermist's Daughter

What is Animal Memorabilia?

I remember ducks in the dryer
I remember wet birds sometimes guts in pails
or Glad garbage bags
I remember mounted voices speaking in tongues
from the basement
I remember wood slats waiting for varnish
I remember squashed grapes lived separate
in the cantina, never mixed with feathers
I remember the freezer keeping meat — a butcher
stocks his rocks of flesh for the feast
I remember playing Persephone hiding
from Hades in abasement
I remember smells of slay in the game
I remember Papa Moose reclining in the sofa
and throning it as his own
I remember arguments with Antlers,
the smug faux Mona Lisa between them
I remember they enjoyed our afterschool conversations
I remember fish flapping in my fingers
I remember the flipped canoe, losing a sneaker,
bottom of the lake
I remember swimming with dragged aluminum —
a whale is hunched over my back
I remember uncles smelly, salty, sweaty and loud
I remember the doorbell, the master's butcher knives
flying around, up and down
I remember the big fish (Pisces) liked to scream
I remember the smelts furious
in the kitchen sink
I remember making friends with turtles

in the backyard
I remember the swish of a bloodied garage
I remember mischief in the Vandura; I don't
remember the automatic shift into drive
I remember rolling forward from the driveway
stopped in a horizontal park, the middle of
you, a trophy
my downward road
I remember dad shouting at the kids
in late summer heat
I remember meeting Polyhymnia's ghost
at the veranda
I remember her applauding an Ace of Cups,
amusing the beast.

Petrarch's Cat, *Sometimes Laura*

A poet is a time mechanic
not an embalmer
— Jack Spicer

Dear friend,

Bring with you, not a prowl, but the tender love of a pacifist,
into the salon where I house my pen. Dreams of her come
with tears I pluck from my heart to wail, *O Carissima!*

Blessed are your purrs in the quiet darkest night.
Stars are a closer proximity when affection is caught from
death's mystery. I have wept watching the trophy
on this desk you return to me every afternoon or evening.

How can I forget? You here, frozen, forever blessed!
We cannot know eternity without love, her whispers,
your whiskers and a warm caress! Both beauty and faith.

The greater flames that burn the heart's passions
are the cause of my soul's unrest, yet when I look
on you, I dare to scribble these tender verses,
in wild abandon to ink exiled from heaven's rest.

What is Taxidermy?

Part 1.
Not including Killing, Cutting, Gutting, Skinning, remove
any natural skin habitat: hair, eyes or such features from
the "specimens" and place each flesh figure over an artificial
standing body made of wood chucks or shavings. Some use
hay squeezed or entangled shaped like footballs with wire
for stuffing. Remember to have plenty of plastic eyes and pins.

Part 2.
The specimen is reproduced completely with man-made
materials. Wipe down gently before skinning then clean
let dry before stuffing, mount bird feet or put antlers,
legs or paws into position.

Part 3.
Taxidermy is not a modern practice, though it has adopted
modern techniques. It is a craft in which carpenters, wood
specialists, rangers and sportsmen advise where the final
pose is a sculpted body. As artifice surfaces, its authenticity
comes with embalming, tanning, moulding and casting.

Part 4.
With a good warm washing, putting together washed out
dead animals, wet with warm water, all evidence of disease
or infection to the human eye is disposed of — the fur,
the skin, the flesh that remains must be dried — blow-dried,
laid flat to dry with an electric heater, in the oven, in a dryer.
All the organs are out and all fatty tissues are disposed of.
Because the most obvious part of the animal of a moose head
are its antlers and the hide becomes an enhanced aesthetic
softening to the human eye, this surface becomes the trophy —
a trope of pride and potential for the hunter's freeze-frame
of time. Sketches, though they come before posing
are like the poet's revisions — an afterlife is created.

Part 5.
The inserted eyes are made from glass, the eyelids are sculpted
from clay, but I've never seen this in my father's workstation.
The noses and mouths are made of clay or wax, sometimes shined,
somehow hardened with a transparent sealer akin to varnish.
I've seen epoxy containers used for shaping mouths. The inside
form is made with foam (polyurethane) or plywood threads
sawed up for stuffing. I've seen these bound up roundish
like a ball of elastics. And for birds, wires and styrofoam hold
together the insides or, as noted above, footballs of shredded
wood strips in place of guts.

Part 6.
Lake fish, sometimes ocean species, are completely gutted
and made with nothing real except fragments of the scale-like
skin. It's important to use gloves. My father doesn't always
follow the rules. He's found his own way of doing things
and I've heard him arguing with my uncle that various
techniques aren't savvy when handling the carcass to
preserve outer layers of skin, hide, feathers or scales.

Part 7.

The standard taxidermy kit consists of special wiring and threads
for markings are precisely cut to make tags. These hold up
wings, legs, and all the various parts of the empty whole to
adjust into position.

The final stages of standing are combined with inserting pins as
support over sanded fancy maple, birch or oak slats are cut and
varnished as a base for the sculpted specimen to 'hold its pose'.

Epilogue

The smell of taxidermy is truly harrowing, more so than watching
these skins lying around. Its stench is a bizarre concoction
of all of the above in various stages — varnish over skin and wet hide.
There are all sorts of tools — screws, pliers, miniature hammers,
an assortment of knives and little scissors. I call taxidermy
a surgical procedure for the dead. A morgue-like ceremony
that evades any necessity for burial. Is it mere showmanship?
Because it is so ostentatious and bizarre for one as conflicted
as myself, the stuffed Armadillo that lives dead-alive, shipped
from Argentina has become one of the few I actually enjoy.

What is Art?

Art
in (taxis) and of translation is coda not a (derma) trope (this is right)

Art
as stuffing but not style (~~this is wrong~~) (this is true)

Art
for posers but not poise (this is right, maybe)

Art
and survival (this is questionable)

Antlers (my favourite) not trophy heads

What is a Modest Livelihood?

A modest livelihood is where dignity and taxis are part of man,
where tents and shacks preserve the piety to meat with man,
or something like that.

(In 2012 Brian Jungen and Duane Linklater hunted together
unsuccessfully for a moose in northern Ontario, in the early
stages of their collaboration on *Modest Livelihood* —
a film which they directed and performed in.)

Similarly, though less serious but equally artistic,
There are about 50 similar, though less serious
VHS films, now CDs, each dated and stored
at the bottom of living room cabinets.

I've called these: docs on hunting and male bonding,
without any previous knowledge of my own hunting capacities.

Recipes

*"Carnal embrace is the practice
of throwing one's arms
around a side of beef."*
— Tom Stoppard

Tenderize

This is what I hear them tell me
from the refrigerator, marinating in milk:
"Our dead bodies want to thirst us."

The second coming of milk is pink, after
butchery comes the onset of rigor mortis.
Keep cool. Refrigerate. Soak in milk, yoghurt,
buttermilk or kefir — the carnage is resting.
This marinating allows for the acids to break
down the toughening, shortened and stiffened
muscle fibres to tenderness.

A Hunter's Gastronomy

I am contaminated yet, contained.
A container of cooked hormones
gnawed into me acidic, a vat of bile
(un)fluid, separated and rejoined for
savoury sustenance and saviour into
nutrient flesh then, theirs excreted
by my ex-communication of excrement.
I eat you. I yam you. I am you —
Hausa nama, carnivorous.

Moose Meat & Puréed Tomato Stew

Grain-cut moose-muscle thick and long
like baby veal slices spread out side by side
placed in a large oval bowl to marinate
in cow's milk, better pasteurized

Refrigerated into milky redness overnight
cold   raw   organic organs
mixed from meat   tenderized
In a large pot sauté onion, garlic, olive oil

The game is fresh, hard — hardly fatty
chopped into square pieces. Let it sizzle
browning on the outside, add red wine
Listen to it fizz to stir in puréed tomato sauce

Stir, stir it like a great brew, the aroma
softer than elk or caribou. Be creative
add basil, thin sliced red peppers, zucchini and salt
Simmer for two hours, keep it steaming hot

A rich tomato moose bourguignon
requires chewing with precision
Like precious stones gone soft
the tissue folds, stouter than beef

Succulent with sauce, the plush life
melts in the mouth
A bite of baguette-roasted garlic
bread to sup the juice

The autumnal heart of a hunter's
catch and feed cooked in truth, I give thanks
to this homeland. The bountiful wilderness
wild-deer, a nourishing cholesterol-free feed.

Moose & Puréed Tomato Stew Recipe

Marinade

2 lbs. moose meat
1 glass white wine
2 cloves garlic chopped with parsley
rosemary
thyme

Ingredients

3 strips pork belly (cut into ½ inch cubes)
2 cloves garlic
salt
pepper
parsley
bay leaves
1 glass white wine
2 glasses beef consommé
1 cup cut carrots (½ inch cubes)
1 cup cut celery (½ inch cubes)
1 cup cut red onion (½ inch cubes)
2 cups puréed tomato sauce

Cooking instructions

Sauté ~~pork~~ belly ~~cubes~~ in a deep skillet until ~~brown~~.
Add ~~meat,~~ salt and pepper. Sauté ~~meat~~ until it's ~~about~~
~~to brown and has~~ absorbed most of the juices.

Sauté   belly   in a deep skillet until
Add   salt and pepper. Sauté   till
    absorbed most of the juices.

Add onions, garlic, chopped parsley and garlic.
Sauté till brown, then add wine and consommé.
Bring meat to a boil, then cook at a low to medium
heat in covered skillet for 1 hour.

Add onions, garlic, *chopped* parsley and garlic.
Sauté till ~~brown~~, then add wine and   consommé.
Add carrots, celery and additional consommé if juices
are completely absorbed, then add 2–3 cups
tomato sauce. Cook for 1 to 2 hours, depending on
toughness ~~of meat~~.

Cervidae

What you eat is what we eat is
what you eat is what we eat with you.

What you chew is what we chew is
what you chew is what we chew with you.

What you swallow is what we swallow is
what you swallow is what we swallow with you.

What you wear is what we wear is
what you wear is what we wear with you.

What you fear is what we fear is
what you fear is what we fear with you.

What you excrete is what we excrete is
what we use to grow grass from you.

*"All flesh is grass, and all the godliness thereof is
as the flower of the field. The grass withereth,
the flower fadeth: because the spirit of the Lord
bloweth upon it; Indeed, the people
(all mammals) are grass."* — Isaiah 40: 6–7

Deer, Elk or Caribou

Ingredients

1 ½ kg boneless meat (cut into 1" or 1 ½ cubes)
3 tablespoons olive oil
1 onion sliced
6 bacon slices finely chopped
3 bay leaves
2 cups beef stock
½ cup cider vinegar
½ cup sherry or port wine
1 cup peeled red pearl onions or white onions
2 carrots (cut in ½" pieces)
2 parsnips (cut in ½" pieces)
1 apple (cut in ½" pieces)
fresh chopped parsley
½ cup whipping cream (35%)
1 tablespoon curry powder
salt
pepper

Cooking instructions

Marinate meat cubes in a large bowl in 2 or 3 glasses of wine
overnight. Season meat with salt and pepper and sauté
in heated olive oil in a Dutch oven frying pan. Add chopped
onion and ½ to 1 tablespoon curry powder. Cook till meat
turns golden, about 6–8 minutes. Add bay leaves, 3–4 cups
hot water, season with salt and pepper as needed and let
simmer for about 40 minutes. Pour in stock, cream, cider
vinegar, sherry or port wine and 1 cup hot water.
Continue simmering for 20 minutes.

While meat is cooking, sauté bacon in another frying pan
till crispy, about 10 minutes. Drain grease from pan,
leave about 2 tablespoons grease in pan. Add red pearl onions,
sauté for a few minutes, then add ½ tablespoon curry.
Sauté for a few more minutes, add carrots and parsnips
and cook till vegetables are wilted. Add salt and pepper.
Garnish with parsley, wilted or raw, before serving.

Wild

bone free
                pluck
hot water weakens the skin
                                                after it's been *shot*
~~the bird has been~~ *shot*   the innards.
                                        the finer feathers are
            like human hairs around the skin.   burned
                        over a gas burner   ignited.
A lighter   in the absence of a gas stove.

                        cut in half at
                mid-breast. Same as   poultry.
                discard head, feet and stomach.
Livers   make a liver paté.

Wash   cut   in quarters
and remove all bones. If   big,
the meat will be tougher. Freeze half and cut the other half
in 1 to 2 inch cubes. The meat of an older _____ is tough,
dry and stringy.   slow cook
for a long time.   A younger _____ is tender
cooking ~~time~~ will be shorter.

This recipe is for an older _____ in relation to ~~cooking~~ time.
The same ingredients are used for a younger ~~one~~ with
fewer steps and   less time.   Marinate~~d~~
overnight or early   morning   the same day.

Wild Turkey

Ingredients

½ boneless ~~turkey~~ (cut into 1–2 inch cubes)
2 glasses white or red wine (6 oz. glass)
4–6 tablespoons olive oil
1 tablespoon butter
4 cloves garlic
5 shallots
generous amount of chopped parsley
rosemary
bay leaves
2–3 cups chicken stock
2 8oz. cups puréed tomato sauce
salt
pepper

Notes

~~This recipe works best if the wild turkey meat is~~ bone free.
~~First step,~~ pluck ~~the feathers with plenty of hot water,~~
hot water weakens the skin ~~around the feathers.~~
~~The longer the feathers stay~~ on a bird after it's been *shot,*
~~the tougher it is to remove its feathers. It is best to it do this~~
~~as soon as~~ the bird has been *shot.* ~~Then remove~~ the innards.
~~This makes the process much easier for~~ the finer feathers are
~~almost~~ like human hairs around the skin. ~~These can be~~ burned
~~by holding the turkey~~ over a gas burner.
A lighter ~~might be an option~~ in the absence of a gas stove.

~~After all feathers are removed~~, cut ~~the turkey~~ in half at the
~~section of the~~ mid-breast. Same as ~~with other~~ poultry.
~~It is of preference to~~ discard the head, feet and stomach.
Livers ~~can be~~ cooked ~~separately to~~ make a liver pâté.

Wash the meat ~~thoroughly~~, cut ~~the turkey~~ in quarters
and remove all the bones. If ~~the turkey is~~ big, ~~this means~~
the meat will be tougher. Freeze half and cut the other half
in 1 to 2 inch cubes. The meat of an older ~~turkey~~ is tough,
dry and stringy. ~~This means the meat has to~~ slow cook
for a long time. ~~The meat of a~~ younger ~~turkey~~ is tender,
~~thus,~~ cooking ~~time~~ will be shorter.

This recipe is for an older ~~turkey~~ in relation to ~~cooking~~ time.
The same ingredients are used for a younger one with
fewer steps ~~and less cooking time~~. ~~Turkey can be~~ marinated
overnight or early in the morning ~~if cooking~~ the same day.

Marinade

Place ~~turkey~~ in a large bowl. On a flat board, mince/chop
2 cloves garlic and parsley, chop 2 shallots with a cutting
knife. In a separate small bowl, add minced garlic and parsley,
shallots, rosemary, 4 tablespoons olive oil and 1 or 2 glasses wine.
Add mixture to meat. Refrigerate till cooking time.

Cooking instructions

Step 1
Put marinated ~~turkey~~ in a cooking pot
with melted butter and hot oil, 2–3 tbsp. Add salt,
pepper and bay leaves if meat is tender (young ~~turkey~~).
Cook on medium to medium-high burner, sauté meat,
cover, stir regularly till marinade has
evaporated and meat is almost golden. If ~~turkey~~ is young,
omit **Step 2.**

Step 2
If meat is very tough, add 2 cups
chicken broth and bay leaves.
Cook at medium-to-low, keep covered.
Stir occasionally till broth has evaporated.

Step 3
While ~~the turkey is~~ cooking, in another small pot
add 3–4 tablespoons olive oil, 2 cloves chopped
garlic, 3 shallots (chopped), sauté till shallots are
wilted but not brown, add puréed tomato sauce,
basil leaves and salt. Let sauce cook slowly
for about 15–20 minutes, stirring regularly.

Step 4
When meat is golden add cooked tomato sauce
~~to the turkey~~ and let simmer for 30 minutes.
To enhance flavour, keep pot covered, simmer and stir.

Roast

Sprinkle   with salt, pepper and rosemary
inside and outside. Put bay leaf, garlic with parsley
and lemon slices in body   Tie legs with
string and place   breast upwards. Place
              onions and mushrooms across breast,
around   Pour   broth over   ~~roast~~
at 350 degrees for 2 hours.   Baste frequently.
For best results, use a covered ~~roasting~~ pan.

Roast Pheasant

Ingredients

1 young pheasant
1 bay leaf
2 cloves garlic minced with parsley
2 shallots or 1 sliced onion
4 to 5 bacon slices
200 gr fresh mushrooms sliced
2 slices lemon
1 cup chicken broth
salt
pepper

Cooking instructions

Sprinkle ~~pheasant~~ with salt, pepper and rosemary
inside and outside. Put bay leaf, garlic with parsley
and lemon slices in body ~~cavity~~. Tie legs with ~~cooking~~
string and place ~~pheasant~~ breast upwards. Place
~~bacon slices~~ across breast, onions and mushrooms
around ~~the bird~~. Pour ~~chicken~~ broth over ~~bird and~~ roast
at 350 degrees for 2 hours. ~~Check and~~ baste frequently.
For best results, use a covered ~~roasting~~ pan.

Friends

Doe

I am learning to *hide*
the hairs of this language
by losing [an] other.

I give you words in all of my skins—
moistened, tanned, stained/stamped
leather   patent or pleather

unplastic   patented.
Suede — each kneaded to still
my style of perfection's needs.

You shall wear these
and them
afraid   friendless.

Advice from a Crying Bear

She drops tears at maple trees
Claws tearing at trunks down *right*
into tree root

She tears at the womb
Sapless
sniffs   meanders   stalks

Her monument frame drops, wears itself
into the unchartered garbage dump

Homing interest
homing disinterest
hers is a drop-dirty disdain

I (can) tear in tears at more
scrupulous stuff
     scruff or sniff
than you, Grizzly.

Elegy for a Stuffed Duck

for Jack and Joe

O Calamus! Let us follow the birds
to paradise in the wild range, its low fielding sky,
turn our backs from the earned science

of con artist structures and vehicle cement
to the call of faraway climes,
where stillness and a one-eyed firearm shot

assembles its avifaunal decree:
Should you get to stirring the wings to seconds from time,
pay attention to the gliding wind; it moves faster than your mind.

O mallards, O ring necks, O wood ducks! We survey
snivel for a closer listen to your clarinet sighs, aim to
silence your swank saxophone quack

Without a pluck we witness those flaps clasp
under atmosphere's ballast
a flop-drop of blown bird brains bereft

Both we are left —
"Have you ever wrestled with a bird, Hunter?"
Us loaded Winchester Nimrods cradling our guns.

Great Canadian White Buck(et)

Walleye

Bass

Catfish

Rainbow Trout

Smelt

Lake Salmon

Riffle-shell

Perch Pike Pickerel

Five-lined Skink Lizard

Gartner Snake & Frog

3 Eels   4 Crayfish

Great North Bucket

Superior bound for

          American guts.

How to Become Friends with the Coyote

On Accounts of the Wounded or A Story of
the Wounded Animal Stalker

When the Shamans (of Ontario) kill the hunter
he becomes the hunted, an alternate voice
having lost his four-legged stolen steps, now two

The coyote has its rite to the body for a bite
Red hots of blood   This is all game
The signature of flesh

He comes home and says to his wife —
*"O Hail Mary! Hail to my lady, I found
Jesus on the trail."*

Nesting with the Sparrow

In the long-ago shadows of our past
I was beneath your ribs, eating foliage

crumbs and twigs from grassy park grounds —
our (re)creation. I was the gorge between

your legs, waiting for the collide of water and womb:
puddles for the sparrow. I was in your mind

perverse or pleasant with no other path *to peace
or please.* Sharing worms, using our '*gossamer wings*'

now nested, I long to return to you. Pardon broken
twigs / hold our dirt / mimic your call/ listen to chatter/

enter the dark world of your Mouth — broken
beaked, beaten, breathing.

My Grating to Hudson

Weary with toil, I haste me to my bed
Cold limestone   Glacial Moraine
Deer me, white-tail   I'm tir'd.
My antlers, limbs tremble at this or thus
from a lacustrine voyage over silt
cascades outside this heaving head.

O how light jaunts
runs — rays alongside my drooped eyelids. *I,*
a perpendicular pilgrim blind   due north
to see-a-sons, lurch and black spruce,
zealous for family at Moosonee.

Whispers up hill, my upper newer hide
rests with grass and soil — I breathe
beauteous wet, ghastly quiet sighs.

This Is Why I Called You Shrimp

Pink skinned baby fat coo coo
spaghetti blonde noodles
      & Shrimp

What's hiding in the kitchen shorter than a table?
Who's tearing up the National Geographic?

4 rows of yellow shelves
"It is so appropriate to be unfound"
whimpers in small steps

around   around   around   and around
you twirl   little deer   dear crustacean

Diapers and doo-wop plop can do us right!

Were we ever lucid?   Golden Harbour curls
Her coast & curves — an Orange County of mucho
melanin — stronger skin.

Jagged rocks squirt from your Pacific eyes
squinting those little irises to a bluer marine

Where you drifting to, Shrimp?
We have the same deferred sun

Did you find the valley girls eating fish tacos?
stucco-stuck under terra cotta tacked slopes

Did you know I thought about you last night?   Again.
Setting those Sagittarius forest fires on the Laguna Hills

1 month + 4 days = 34 days + my 7 years

Scurry Sister Chick Over My Hen Mama
I called for you   Shrimp
Sonia's just the   Cocktail
Didn't you know?

Whale Revenge

Dreadful waterways that collapse
over reefs, under glacial rifts.
Her curve moves into icy seas.

A noose for her nose, her stoic hole.
The watery node opens,
shoots from its splint whole.

Spray touching sky, 52 ft. upward,
her waterway fountain hauls
direct into concave.

A weight for whiter waters,
then lapping, shiny smooth skin,
a rubbery roof — she shouts

hooved sounds,
wailing water-wish
from whalebones.

Greener

The Greening Heart

for Hildegard

The whiter roots gleam. Their vessels

orbit the ground, greening virtuous sprouts.

She's indexed the 'Green finger of God'

to Glory — a light in spaces or places.

Those aces between words and worlds, sounding

to Sappho's lyre: *"I am greener than grass ..."*

"Viriditas Gloriosa," she, a foundling, chants theorems

in her virile garden. And when it rains water with acid tears,

She cries a prayer to the Greener — listens for leafy openings

to her Ordo Virtutum when she writes, "Let's not call it poison

but a metallurgical decay — a chlorophyll florescence".

Stems and Valves

Let   her

Letting

I,

Let   me

Let   me   in

                    Heart

Letting   blood   circle

in   out —   in   out —   valve

out let me.

Let   me   give

Let me give   words   words

Give   worlds

Let me give words to (y)our visions.

circulate   in

circulate   out

                                        out/let

Hilde and I

[Scito vias Domini]

Know   the   ways
of
Your Lord.

Patriarchs   &   Prophets

Who   are   these

Goats   or   Gods?

[above   clouds]

Who are they

that gloat

above clouds?

Sinking into Savanna

In bottomland, its hardwood junctions made soft
Comes refuge where that is all you know —
There is no shelter in a sojourn
when brown bubbles into the breath.

Pollinators hide in Savanna swings,
bumbling their wings but you've never been
spinning buoy over bayou. Swamps making
friends with the American Alligator.

Her children hide in the greening marsh —
a muddied fire-water. You submit your flesh,
correspond, afraid of becoming a boil. You'd
rather drown red-thick without dragon wingspans

Stick to submerging sweat as the rods of growing
trunks suck into you slow. He'll come for you wild
as Loblolly Pine when the light is low, ignore the
comely candelabras, their yellow glow.

The heat cuts longleaf at your Godspell bible soul.
He sifts, plucks at the perfumes of green decay,
forced to panting you swell for home. Still,
the slimy nostril stems fight and blow.

Our (eco) Shit & Our (fading) Green Trousers

Not honey, not jam. Campfires — crackling.
Was it a burn? A skin-crimped blister about to pop?

Orange trees grow lust — that doesn't
happen here. The watermelons emigrate,
count out their wound-patterned seedlings
losing sugar juice.

O'er for an order to ecology like wham poles we fuck.
'Tis a-wash-away sorrow, sweet with your sweat,
shit, my green trousers. Or my shit and your

Green trousers. Together we dance dank —
our hair, our eyes, our lips become lookalikes
navigating the confused compass.

Crashing our ships leaving knots and wrecks, our
salty skins — foamier sea-white lilies drowning

to keep a Shallow Depending Home.
Were the 1980s a friend to anyone
or just another neon romance?

Camaraderie

The quiet Fleur-de-lys
sprout a warning
of the sovereign knot —
My knotted Francophone friend,
bearing her necklace, its charm
this 400th weekend, 24th of June.

Marie de Medici isn't eager
to cross these icy skins, our lapping
ocean and rivers that hide

poison ivy in spring
(among fern ghettos)
          over granite
          over ore.

Shield shelved into rock,
this greener ground
(jewels of silver
amber   quartz)
cast under Champlain's shores —
Temiskaming and Ville Marie.

Our kindred bovinae spirits —
Wilder-ness-Miss Buffalo   exiled.
Reproducing nil, we wile
trampling trilliums.
Frayed grass flowers align
between province and providence.

In blood, we draw iron from these plants
that seep it out of soil — we are
diagnosed with mineral deficiency.
Our *"teeth and bones, once coral"*
now white, the ovaries turned to fluorite.

A Golden Hunger Trails the Emerald City

A shadowy portrait sits 123° 22' West, 48° 25' North
Emily Carr by satellite. Her fist pinches at short dry grass,
sluices the earthy canvas as if it were jelly.

Her fingers are yellow dandelions.
They know the brush of wise weeds,
conversations with friendly firs, abundant trees.

She takes pollen-stained notes
watching the pliable growth quiver
with maples in afternoon wind —

A row of cedars speak in tongues,
"Ah, what's for dinner?
I am coming out of mourning."

Toward the Emerald city everyone bends
pine-like wanting kindness,
more matcha, green tea.

At dusk, there is an aroma of oak and oils
mixed in trails toward greener glass towers
sunning the sky, rays lick climbing shiny gilded easel walls.

This Bus Rides North

Pick (me) up trucks
over endless road way
wanting time travel.
How do we knead national largeness?

Away city — crowded pavements
drowning in sky haze,
the horizontal of bus hum;
bush-whacked road

rails without killdeer.
A musical movement in
window lapse,
pine and birch birth,

crow bytes, tree sprawl
straighter sun rays sting.
Looking through the clouds
a fever, touch sky, ridged granite,

farmhouses abandoned
in shadow and green séance.
Black water lake welcome,
entering   entering

(my)   North on high.

American Cliché

And taking the road, yonder —
without the tears of Hollywood
or 1985, Thelma & Louise snuffed out.
Inanna and sister dancing at the cliff, but

there aren't any edges here, just dry
dust and my underworld of underwear,
the car's oil spilled, walking
into the Nevada brown, no, red! not brown

earth, one jug left bearing the grace of.
Without water where rain doesn't know its tears.
No one goes down together here for
better or worse — just(ice) melted/drained

dis-jointed/discombobulate/disembodied
parts/wheels deflated,
stationed-in-the-hot-horizon — just parts:
mufflers/eroded metal/loose strings,

the-spit-on-the-rock-heat.
Olson's "America is just a complex of occasions"
Hitch   ride   stop
A heated heart at the nearest Texaco station.

Red Colossus

after Sylvia Plath, Colossus

I shall never get you put together entirely.
Han dynasties — pieced, glued, improperly jointed.
Tiger prowls, mule-bravery, pig-grunts and Monkey King's
bawdy cackles. All of it hushed by great lotus lips and a
monk's moon, an eclectic expanse of rickety barnyards,

bold reign ruins among silken worms of women in silence.
A kingdom considers itself a Confucian Oracle when
workers labour, do not dread the dredge into unbreathable
limestone and silt, raise themselves up to Mao, the monumental
Red throat, its tiny soft ma — mouthpieces that sing of the
    Dragon.

Bamboo scaffolds become ladders, they lift concrete and glass
by camouflaged workers, the praying-mantis is dewed in
    mourning.
I want to stretch upward, sway over immense constructs, climb,
bend with thin trunks and weedy acres — arrive to cleave at
Buddha's half-smile.

A failed Manchu emperor and his son's ghost are seated,
sealed hostage in the Palace like Forbidden frogs,
a billion proud stars stomp over red gravitas. It would take
more than a Great #Firewall to break this mass, the flouted
bones and black hair sand-packed between stone.

Echoes weep, *Meng Jiangnü* is in the Mutianyu mist.
Her horizon travels east, smaller into the hidden sun. Under
the pillars and ridges of crying tongues live too many years
marred by past shadows, plum-coloured orchids.
I am beckoned by iPhones and karaoke romance,

westward bound. Salivating for entanglements with
the rice noodle. Early in the party morning, I slurp,
chew into the dumpling, I float wanton
into a peasant mother's womb. I listen
for the scrape of jade bracelets on my wrist,
I suck at the dragon fruit, hum at taste,
I get a succulent bite of this Colossal blood.

Who Dares to Encounter
the Dragonfly of Binhai?

At a crossroads we intersect, you greet me, ask,
"Which way shall I go or will you follow? I've been here
eons, though recently, I have come into thinking
I'm sometimes lost. This is all a familiar (a)new."

Navigating your thousand years among the recent human
ballast of stones in angular noise, you continue to seek out
weeping willows for a gentle hook into the sway of breeze.

My unexpected, unconsidered, friend? of the seaside city
who whirls its visit among planned urban spaces —
fresh silt and sediment. Have you circled yourself enough today?

Flit Hebei of its newly grouted terrain?
I am introduced to you, these first footsteps
over cubed granites, limestones, marbles.

I see you dwell between Binhai Area Shadows
of Structure and the Sun's Rays. The Mortar bare —
bearing your venerable ancient sentience.
Who knew the predator changes form, arrives miniature

among the forewarnings of colossal dragons where
the pruned roses don't care much on any given day.
It's humid and they are thirstier than you.

I hear your wings speaking in tongues seeking warm winds,
lifting high, then low with the musical honk of moving
humans driving past. You've a heavy-hearted concrete
competition among cemented stone.

Odonata, the regal larger larvae of an Insect Kingdom,
flits between firmament and cement — moving horizontal
with Taller Standing Towers — erect to Yang, out of earth's still Yin.

Penetrated human emblems: mixed earth skyscrapers —
granite, marble, limestone — aggregates, each boulder
bound for the arrival of a true romance.

Greetings to *the Dragonfly of Binhai* — In downtown *TEDA district*,
my dominion and your domain bring us closer at the knees of
a shortening sky, scanning low — not above some human head,
reaching up between the eyes.

Hands on World

~~I'm out~~   *of* Orion

a little Swan

Silent
Leda-like   in lakes

a stillness   in orbits   *of* Orchids

laden   lasting

my scents   white *or* blackened

~~troubles~~   truffles.

Both hands keep symbiosis
their rattled grip on lawnmowers
fingers hovering underneath
dawn, nails jutted out   *to* scrape
against soiling dis-ease.

My palms holding   ~~out for~~

St. Agnes.

The Moon
and Her Friends

*Darlings, I speak to you on
high 'over the moon,' with a
silvered crest I shine, sometimes
black, sometimes white as the
frost on windowpanes.*

Moon Madness

Another round to make the world nauseous
full, a complete ambition opposite to

a bull, hangs under the sky in Taurus, clarifies
grey matter. It's a task to watch you well,

though it helps to know you're less uprooted
for this month's rotation   much like my own

moon-shaped medicine, what I take each day
to make more serotonin for moon-white

phases that record soul wave sadness, tell
it to swell, at each full or new moon that

moves round year by year. How sweet
it is that memory hurts because brainwaves

speak to brainstems saying *such dis-ease is
not a limbic roundabout glow.*

On Keeping an Angel in the House

She thrashes about confused

whimpering at
the flowers

limping with
the machine-cut meat

openings in
the skin

shedding at
renewal in the room

clamouring at
mismatched routine

frowning to
the moon

floating with
dizzy glee

dancing with
woven wings

trying to flap
outside the ceiling.

Walking with the Mob

It took her decades to understand a Godfather. The declaration
of a 'Don', why men like to make arrangements for money

and kill for a share of minced meat, of glory, of guts,
of gutter deals. When there's nothing left to live for

the extra buck of the day — What's to lose? Perhaps too much
family and too much love, all that's too hard to live for,

all that's been done. There's an infamous quote from a Roman
Senate politician, *"Rome is the Mob. Give them the Gladiator,*

you'll give them glory." In the last decade, she awakens
after an incoherent lapse of identity. Returns to reruns

of Coppola's Godfather. She has been at that party with the
projector camera, reels of father's films on her skin. She visits

on occasions with The Sopranos, Boardwalk Empire,
Road to Perdition. At Christmas toasts to familiar days

she gathers with Hollywood's obsession, makes it her own.
Uncles built like mobsters and their entourage gnomes. She

once scoffed at stories of organized crime, those stereotypes
far from Canadian-born ethics, away with Shakespeare,

Beckett and Chekov. She tries to save herself, naïve to
the clever pathos of thugs and guns. There's always some

reunion to remind each of us about days long gone in a high
school we'd forgot, at a gathering to gossip with familiars,

old friends that show us more of ourselves, what lies beneath
the daily village. Pals and cousins are a reminder — she sees

herself Catholic and colonial in a ghetto of women with whom
therapy is an ongoing village waltz. The perfect Don's daughter.

The perfect Mob wife. The Juliet of every epoch. Her friend
who disappeared over two decades ago. A young woman returns

to Sicily by choice or destiny to know both in a life of marriage.
Her faith is a sacrificial roll-call by ancient patriarchs of

Columbus moving west. A child that leaves parents and siblings
from this ocean, a return to her matron's walk with the mob that

came before cowboys, corporate layoffs, oil among oceans
to a terroir that's certain—murders in cold blood. She knows

hers is a christened wealth steeped in marble where thousands
of year-old passions reign and roses for women grow wild

at villa gates, unpruned stems and sharp thorns. Piracy,
both a crime and justice, an equality that cannot exist.

Her dad says, "half a century ago I left home because of
corruption." Such is the friendship of two school girls like men.

She, audacious for a matriarchy, her friend—a free-born brat
(or bitch) serving poets and politics, listening to gangsters,

watching followers, disobedient priests, bearing some childhood
innocence that lies cherished in pathos. America's myth, status,

triumphs and films. Soldiers or spies, the drops are private and
personal truths. She admires these typecasts: Pacino, De Niro,

Gandolfini and Hardy. She sinks in with their storied red
quicksand, learns to love it, becomes one with Capone,

Canadian whiskey, Kennedys' bootlegs, Sinatra's wrongs.
She knows assaults and violence are the manners of hubris

and a sad hypocrite singing songs to the gambler, the drug
trafficker—those donkeys of a different age. She's stepped in,

wants to bear this life worth living, its anger worth taking
because without Brutus and Caesar, there is no anxiety
of death or the mundane.

See Something Black to See Something White

Whitewashed walls named White Dove.
　　A Sanctuary of Space.

A purple glass vase with a neckline of tightly wound
aluminum coils. Handpicked Black-eyed Susans
　　sing yellow bright.

On a pinewood desk basil and parsley stems drown
in a glass cylinder. A wall mirror hangs between

two closet doors. Upwards from the floor, a short square
mirror leans back, stout and wide. Seafoam plastic

flip-flops on a crooked Persian rug patterns from silk —
　　smiles a miniature white Tara Buddha.

　　We are having a conversation in silence.

　　　　　　　　　*

In 1981, I was selected *flower girl* for auntie's
old world Catholic Italian-Canadian wedding.

In those days Toronto was The Six6,
this neighbourhood — North York,

all the bridesmaids and the bride spent two days
stringing together *fake flowers* from Kleenex

or Charmin toilet paper. Women in bellbottoms
hanging out in Nonna's kitchen giddy for the party.

Apart from paper airplanes in class, this was
my first introduction to the ornate work of folding

and unfolding paper, delicate and Origami-like.
We made at least 60 to decorate each of the 'stag' cars,

the sport Mazda, the sport Mustang, a Corvette and
a Pinto. The morning of, all eyes on me, I followed

the bride holding a small bouquet of white roses.
I glided down the veranda, from the supposed
Stairway to Heaven, a Princess in White.

*

By '84 my aunt and uncle divorced.
I ripped my chiffon white dress,

stained it with chlorophyll and dirt,
blackened my socks as I tumbled about

in James Edwards Gardens with little cousins
refusing to take pretty pictures for Dad.

At dinner, I lost my shoes underneath
the bridal party table.

By 9 pm, the DJ blared Sister Sledge,
"We are Family", I was punch-face drunk

on broken English conversation
and cantina homemade red wine.

Tipsy

Darling, you will yield up your belly and be
behind my eye.
Let's cry a little while
as if we are at a movie
and the quinces and kisses are glowing
the night of deep dreams. Though sometimes I float
& my pace appears rippling.

Sizzle the Cold Earth

The garden has a cold cucumber and a wilting tomato
that no longer grows before the now twilight — 6 pm

when the sun commanded the arrival of an autumnal wind,
I wanted us to take a barefoot walk, salient to the senses,

in the neighbourhood park, feel a touch of vanishing warmth
on our cheeky smiles — a sweet nearby, before the chill

starts a chat. There's no sense in evading it, there's a bottle
of *Amarone* red at my hip and tea tree oil for our bare feet.

Minty cool earth conversation   frisk skins   a cotton sack
that's black with words   a line drawing of a woman

round and nude — let's deal with it. We're going cold wild.
Dig it, dude. The day is not long gone. Sizzle the cold earth,

this true north strong and free, that's what I long to find
some crisp inhuman chill where the lungs go shrill and the first

peoples laugh because we haven't got a clue how to make both
blood and breath a toast to soul.

Luna Bound

This wit-warm womb peeks out, first
to grow tentacles from a dark vessel
evading space debris

I come, Luna bound, brave,
my bounce a touch of dust
in dirt-dry elements —

they blow upward at non-gravity,
wound with empty craters.
Hellas basin is the first to hear

my delayed arrival in waves
to you, moon, a wound
wound in your own evening.
Sunlight and dark of earth-day —

you, moon, my rounder egg,
we are a non-encounter.

Moon Mirage

i could never understand why
they call it *Skinny Dipping*

my clever guess — water is amorphous
it liquefies human form
at any vantage point

you can see parts of me
you do not know all of me

      shapes   splash
disperse   disappear
      reappear   release
rotate   ripple
      sink   float

wet, naked and nude, why
does civilization fool itself?

      illusory   adrift

my legs and torso reduced
to a vulnerable amphibian
lungs grasping at air

i am desperate
i am shy
i want to dive down

ask you to come closer
warm me   under lake water
dipped skins gone soft.

The Wonder of Mind Loss at a Degree

this tide is a windfall breaking backwards
this omen is a singing sky-crack in wonder
this mother is a pit against anxiety in the heart
this goddess salad dressing chews cool and crisp
this century arrives in an increase of heat
by 1°

this skin is a natural disaster deliciously charred
this brick is a boring morbid clutter of sediment
this toe is a beacon for my being alone and alive
this march is an unwanted drum for common sense
this corner probes at some dimension for escape
                    this is a test by 1°

this child is a pilgrimage in pardon each evening
this time is a forfeit of presence lost to tic toc
this breast can grow its shape by quantum formulas
this anaesthetic makes a miracle of disappearance
this tin holds tinkers for a desk that wants more room
                         the messages by 1°

Moonflower

I see it hide among greenleaf castles where
I can't tell between bedtime and late show-time.
The Honeymooners   I love Lucy   Judge Judy

Nonna laughs loud   hard like a vigilante
            drinking tea in the afternoon
gets hungry late at night   looks for cold food
in the fridge   she smells   the nightmares
at the window   silvery shine mushroom hair
she is a tousled zombie   a crackled flesh
out of the sheets — an aegis wiles
while the world holds the spectre of scales.

Anubis never left or vanished with the sand.
He's up close to the ground   weighing hearts.
Archaeologists say Set was a greedy son;
beyond the grave he lost gravity of mind.
The doctor can't have given her enough pills,

she's already popped
what great God couldn't have warned us —
the needles for tetanus, polio and pox.
A working class post-war memory foam,
slimy coins slipping out of pockets.

The politely placed paper in broken wallets,
best friends with plastic holding the merry-
go-round until she'll collapse from a headless
turning trauma   music-box sounds   drop down.
Love pays (demon)itized, like a capital punishment.

My ancestor who dwells at the local strip-mall
fair, a candid candied apple consumer accounted
for elder, an under-worthling gone soft —
moon spent by purpose and purposelessness.

Return to the Moon

after Giacomo Leopardi, Alla Luna

My DNA village cannot include everyone.
It cannot be enough no matter if the year has turned.

I find an empty castle in dust and stone,
the graceful ghost of an artist full of anguish.

Oil paintings hang as if we could float above
these hills I've wanted to call my own.

I came here to gaze at memories —
what I can remember I enter   a lost key,

cloudy faces hanging from portraits like stones
that no longer welcome me.

I want the homes made of rock and hay
to have said, "O she's back to join us, sit

at the fountain with her shine and shadow,
talk with distant cousins by day,

dead ancestors by night."
No one in this town recognizes me,

the voices in the piazza hush as I arrive.
There's never been a place to begin.

I visit the foothills   find the mausoleum,
look for her   some uncles   some aunts,

great grandparents among the twilight.
I do not find her   there are too many

new graves. I look up to the untamed grass
slope, it offers its protection, makes its way

facing souls in the light of a crescent glow
and shadow *sovra questo colle*   I talk with you.

Invitation

I invited you over
for pasta for wine for pot for tea for sex for fruit
you weren't interested in the food just flesh talk
without a mouth   wine becomes water
perhaps each liquid is a unique glory — a mood music
perceives gravity   they say for some food is sex
but I say *it's a Bildingsroman* to savoury tongues
over throats gone dancing with flavour buds.
As long as you don't mope too much
there's no disease in getting fatter   round is love
I eat mooncakes   I eat paper   neither is good for
my bones don't want silence, they want loud ears
and words that mean '*dolce far niente.*'

La Luna at Letter 12

Liberty has me longing

Low has me lingering

Loud has me lapsing

Liquid has me in libation

Lush has me in lustre

Loss has me out of lift

Latitude has me crossed with Longitude

Lime has me loved by lemons

Lady has me underneath languid

Language has me in locution

Large has me fly with locusts

Lard has me lubed

Light has me visited by loops

Lonely has me beside a lamp

Lost has me looking for a label

Lake has me lapping

Liberal has me lorded

Limping has me leaving

List has me lopsided

Leaning has me laughing

Love has me lasting.

Throw All Your Books into the Ocean

> *walking in the dark*
> *waking in dark the presence of all*
> *the absences we have known.*   *Oceans.*
>   *so we are distinguished to ourselves*
> — Phyllis Webb, *Naked Poems*

A radical harmony, like Stravinsky,
flings books into an ocean,
wants pulp to scatter by command.

Maddened by salt, then drowned in sand,
the ink first drips into black oily drops,
waddles like a jellyfish to the skin for a sting.

Spines float inches near shore,
wet words make waves with the surf,
drift for continents, flip over currents.

Once dry-pressed tree trunks
made smooth pages, sap-thick with letters,
bittersweet pageants flowed into language.

Now soaked, begging at descent, they whirl
toward destruction, swallowed and silenced
at the celebration of release.

Throw all your books into the ocean!
Afternoon comes as morning ends
by night, these veins swim with sharks
and sentences are written in blood.

Fleshing

"Shivers whistle when the skin sighs or" "Moonskin"
"or bring into smooth harmony" "or bring on hum",
 "or dare touch" "or squeeze" "and touch is grasp"
"and grasp or squish" "no, not that, only grasp"
"un-touch" "with tangled rhythms, taps" "tapped"
"or tapping" "or trans...pose" "or hairs rise" "or bumps"
"and not transcend this movement" "and keep sense"
"or smooth with the body" "of body," "bodily dance,
not dance" "body grace," "body flutter", "out of the body"
"in" "inside" "side" "of body" "to the body"
"forensic" "or flourish" "fleshing"

Notes

Akashic is derivative of the Hindu & Sanskrit words: Akasha, Akasa or Akash. The 19th century western philosophical Theosophy movement, initiated by Madame Blavatsky, created a term called the 'Akashic Records' or the 'Akashic Library' referring to an ethereal infinite space of knowledge. Akasa or Akash (*Hindu & Buddhist theology*) is the term for 'aether' in the traditional Indian cosmology. Also referring to sky, boundless space and sound. Akash (ether) is considered the first element created from the astral plane to join the material world before the four elements: water, air, earth, and fire; it is the first of five elements, although one that cannot be perceived because of its infinite space and timelessness. In some Buddhist schools, Akasha lives between limited space and endless space.

The Akashic Wood, sections I and III inspired by the lyrics of the song *Ya Hey* by Vampire Weekend

"Why should we hurry home?" — a line from Lorine Neidecker's poem Lake Superior

Samnites* are a population of ancient warlike tribes inhabiting the surrounding areas of the Roman Empire. Prior to Rome's eventual defeat of the central mountainous region in Italy, it was named Sabinum, later Samnium. The south of Italy they referred to as Latium. These tribes who spoke Oscan, an offshoot of inhabitants beyond Pompeii, are named Sabini (*Oscan, similar to Latin*), called Sabines or Samnites (*English*) or Sanniti (*Italian*). Hence, the infamous tale of Romulus summoning the Rape of the Sabine Women. The Samnites, among Romans, were reputed to be tough, non-urban, barbaric and primitive. Although, allied with the Romans against the Gauls in 354 BC, the Samnites were soon involved in a series of three wars against the Romans from 343–290 BC. In June 2004, archaeologists in Pompeii discovered the remains of a wall from a temple built by Samnites. In various populated regions beyond Rome and Pompeii, artifacts and forums are found bearing Latin/Oscan inscriptions with the name of Samnium.

Bonomelli*, a brand of Chamomile tea imported from Italy.

American Spelling (American SP)

Scratched out (...) familiar territory, a line inspired by Jack Spicer's letters to Lorca

Intaglio, an engraved design or figure impressed into hard material or stone.

Vandura, the model name of the Chevrolet Van in the early 1980s prior to the inception of the Mini-Van

Polyhymnia, the muse of sacred poetry, hymn, dance, agriculture in Classical Greece evoking a demeanour of eloquence.

Petrarch's Cat, *Sometimes Laura*

[1]*O Carissima!*

I call this an Amuse Faux Bouche, The Taxidermist's Cantos or The Poet's Free Failure in Translation.

"Strict metrical translators still exist. They seem to live in a pure world untouched by contemporary poetry. Their difficulties are bold and honest, but they are taxidermists, not poets, and their poems are likely to be stuffed birds. A better strategy would seem to be the now fashionable translations into free or irregular verse. Yet this method turns out a sprawl of langue neither faithful nor distinguished, now on stilts, now low, as Dryden would say ... I believe that poetic translation — I would call it imitation — must be expert and inspired and needs at least much technique, luck and rightness of hand as an original Poem." Preface to Imitations, Robert Lowell, 1961

[2] *Trophy*

"During my years as an art critic, I used to joke that museums love artists the way that taxidermists love deer, and something of that desire to secure, to stabilize, to render certain and definite the open-ended, nebulous, and adventurous work of artists is present in many who work in that confinement sometimes called the art world." Rebecca Solnit, Men Explain Things to Me, Essays — "Woolf's Darkness: Embracing the Inexplicable," 2008–14.

Taxidermy is a word joined by two Greek words: **Taxis** and **Derma**. When the two words are combined they translate as the arrangement of an organism with some kind of stimulus that turns away from or moves toward something, with 'derma' this word becomes an arrangement of skin or hide.

Modest Livelihood is an Indigenous film created by Bruce Jungen and Duanne Linklater. It was shown as an exhibit at the Art Gallery of Ontario in 2012.

Recipes developed with the assistance of Antonietta Conte.

Elegy for A Stuffed Duck is for Jack Spicer, Angelo Di Placido and Joe Mancino.

Calamus is the quill of a feather. It is also the English spelling denoting Kalamos, a storied figure in Classical Greece who was turned into a reed after drowning. The etymological history is a word and name derived and altered in African and Middle Eastern languages to describe a reed or quill as writing pen.

Gossamer is italicized because it is a popular word often used to emphasize beauty and romantic ideation by the Romanticist poets Keats and Byron.

"Weary with toil (...) to my bed" First stanza opens with the line from Shakespeare's Sonnet XXVII. My Grating to Hudson is inspired by Ted Berrigan's notion of writing cube poems as the possible modern rendition of a Sonnet.

This is Why I Called You Shrimp is for Laura Di Placido inspired by some of Joanne Kyger's poems referencing the Southern California coastline.

"Green Finger of God", Hildegard Von Bingen often used this phrase in her notes and when she spoke to exemplify that a good balance of green among nature and her surroundings is a vision of being christened by God's index finger, which must be green.

Viriditas Gloriosa, a phrase meaning *"The Glorious Virility"* or "What is virile is glorious." She named and often wrote about this term in reference to her beliefs as to how humanity can maintain well-being and good health both physically and spiritually. The phrase became a philosophical notion which decreed that in virile green there is cause for celebration and glory for life and God.

Ordo Virtutum, a musical play written by Hildegard Von Bingen.

Scito Vias Domini, *Latin* for Know the Ways of The Lord.

Loblolly Pine, a tree family of softwood found in the Southeastern United States

Candelabras, bushes or shrubs also called Candle Bush or

Empress Candle found in Southeastern regions of the United States: Alabama, Arizona, Texas.

Camaraderie is for Julie Carrier. The **24ᵗʰ of June**, Le Fête National du Québec.

"teeth and bones (...) coral" a line by Lorine Niedecker, Lake Superior.

123° 22' West, 48° 25' North is the latitude and longitude, which intersects at Victoria, Vancouver Island where Emily Carr lived.

"America is (...) occasions" a line by Charles Olson, The Maximus Poems

Red Colossus is written after Sylvia Plath's poem Colossus.

Binhai is a suburban city district of Tianjin, China that makes up the coastal plain bay of the Bohai Sea, also known as the Yellow Sea.

Odonata, *Spanish.* The originating name of carnivorous insects, namely the dragonfly family.

St. Agnes of Rome martyred herself to early Christianity at 12 years of age. She refused any other destiny but to remain in servitude to early Christian belief and ritual through the vow of chastity. Because Agnes came from nobility, she was killed publicly in 304 AD. It's speculated she was raped and murdered by the Romans before her death in defiance of her choice to stay devout to Jesus. She is called the Virgin-Saint as she is the youngest Saint christened by the Vatican. She is always depicted with a Lamb in her arms because of her chastity and the meaning of her name being purity. St. Agnes' patronage represents and honours innocence, chastity, purity, gardeners, girls, engaged couples and rape survivors.

On Keeping an Angel in the House is adapted from Virginia Woolf's essay, Killing The Angel in The House

Tipsy is a Cento. Phrases/lines adapted by Anne Sexton, Frank O'Hara, Elise Partridge, Giacomo Leopardi.

Amarone is the name of various blends of thick, rich dry red wines that are also part of the Valpolicella family region of red wines made near Veneto in northern region of Italy.

Moonflower is for Domenica Conte.

sovra questo colle is a line from Giacomo Leopardi's poem Alla Luna, *transl.*
over this hill or over this peak

dolce far niente, a popular Italian phrase meaning *the sweetness of doing nothing — to languish* or be idle without feelings of laziness or boredom. It's recognized as the poetic sentiment adopted by the Romantic poets.

Fleshing is a piece in the manner of Alice Notley's poem The Descent of Allette, Book III.

Acknowledgements

Thanks to:

The editors of The White Wall Review #38, 2014–15 for publishing 7 poems in this collection: *This Bus Rides North, Wine Tasting, American Cliché, Doe, My Grating to Hudson* and *Whale Revenge*

Canthius Journal editors, Cira Nickel and Claire Farley, for publishing two of my poems from this collection in their debut issue. *A Golden Hunger Trails the Emerald City* and *How to Become Friends with the Coyote.*

The Puritan Magazine for the publication of my poem, *Hands on World* with an audio recording, Winter 2014 issue.

The Association of Italian Canadian Writers Editorial for publishing earlier versions of *Hands on World* and *Americas Fatherland*, now known as *The Akashic Wood*, 2014–2016.

The following Poetry Anthology editors: Lillian Necakov, The Boneshaker Reading Series Anthology, 2013 and to Venera Fazio with Delia De Santis, editors of Exploring Voice: Italian Canadian Female Writers, Special Issue of Italian Canadiana, Vol. 30, 2016 for publishing The Akashic Wood poems in their first stages, now complete in this collection.

Lisa Young of Juniper Poetry Magazine for her advice, support and the publication of *Who Dares to Encounter the Dragonfly of Binhai?* in her debut issue, Summer 2017.

Robin Richardson and Minola Review, Issue 18 for featuring my poem *Sizzle the Cold Earth.*

A Big Thanks to Luciano Iacobelli's Lyricalmyrical chapbook imprint for the publication of *The Akashic Wood*, Spring 2016, as well as to Quattro Books and Guernica Editions for their support with The Ontario Arts Council, Writer's Reserve Grants, 2016.

With sincere thanks to Dale Martin Smith and Hoa Nguyen for their dedication to poetry including the workshops and recurring reading series, 2013–.

Thanks to The University of British Columbia, Poetry instructor Ian Williams, fellow classmates and Jim Johnstone for his encouragement.

A final *'tip of the hat'* to friends and family overall. Thank you to The Ontario Arts Council, my editor Elana Wolff and Michael Mirolla with Connie McParland — publishers of Guernica Editions.

About the Author

Sonia Di Placido is currently completing an MFA in Creative Writing at UBC. She is a recurring member of The League of Canadian Poets, The Writer's Union of Canada, The Canadian Women in The Literary Arts and The Association of Italian-Canadian Writers. An Associate Editor of *Juniper Poetry Magazine*, she has poems published by *Carousel, The Puritan, The White Wall Review, Jacket2, Canthius, The California Journal of Women Writers,* and *Juniper Poetry Magazine.* In September 2016, she was part of the *China Writers Association International Writer's Residency* for the cities of Tianjin, Binhai and Beijing. Sonia teaches English as a Second Language with LINC Ontario part-time. Her first book *Exaltation in Cadmium Red* was published with Guernica Editions in 2012. *Flesh* is her second full-length book of poetry.

MIX
Paper from
responsible sources
FSC® C100212

Printed in July 2018
by Gauvin Press,
Gatineau, Québec